Customs Around the

HOMES Around the World

by Wil Mara

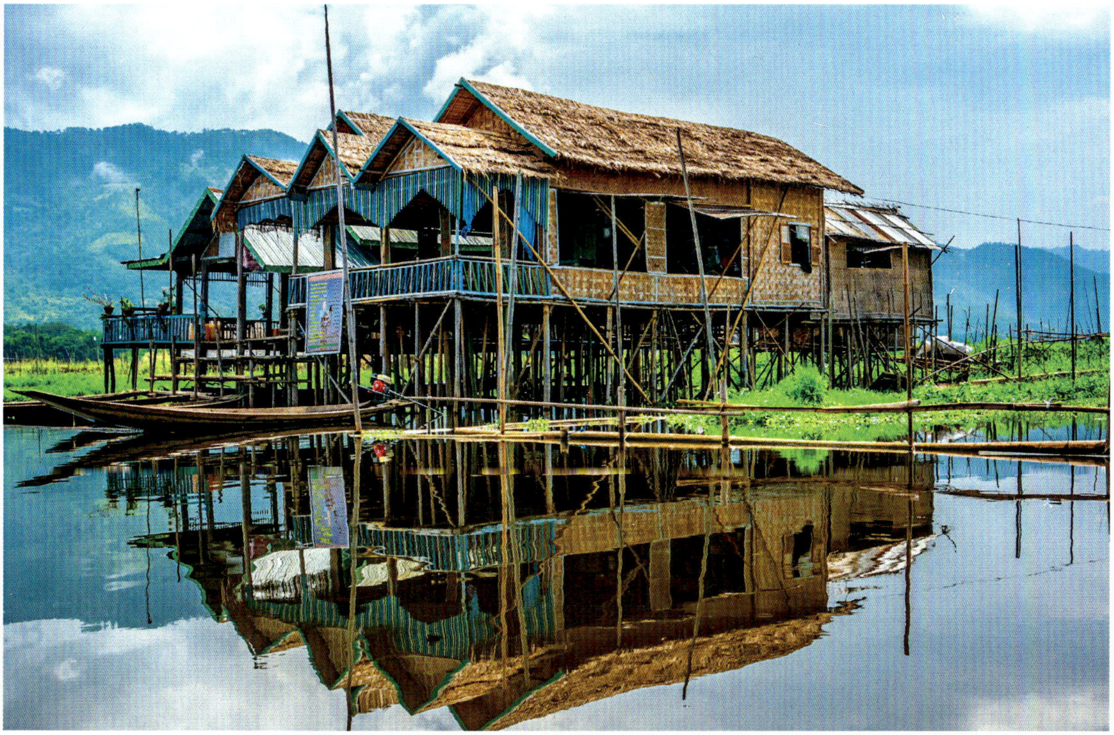

raintree
a Capstone company — publishers for children

Raintree is an imprint of Capstone Global Library Limited, a company incorporated in England and Wales having its registered office at 264 Banbury Road, Oxford, OX2 7DY – Registered company number: 6695582

www.raintree.co.uk
myorders@raintree.co.uk

Text © Capstone Global Library Limited 2022
The moral rights of the proprietor have been asserted.

All rights reserved. No part of this publication may be reproduced in any form or by any means (including photocopying or storing it in any medium by electronic means and whether or not transiently or incidentally to some other use of this publication) without the written permission of the copyright owner, except in accordance with the provisions of the Copyright, Designs and Patents Act 1988 or under the terms of a licence issued by the Copyright Licensing Agency, 5th Floor, Shackleton House, 4 Battle Bridge Lane, London SE1 2HX (www.cla.co.uk). Applications for the copyright owner's written permission should be addressed to the publisher.

Edited by Abby Huff
Designed by Julie Peters
Original illustrations © Capstone Global Library Limited 2022
Picture research by Jo Miller
Production by Spencer Rosio
Originated by Capstone Global Library Ltd
Printed and bound in the United Kingdom

978 1 3982 0264 1 (hardback)
978 1 3982 0263 4 (paperback)

British Library Cataloguing in Publication Data
A full catalogue record for this book is available from the British Library.

Acknowledgements
We would like to thank the following for permission to reproduce photographs: Getty Images: Mark Kolbe/Staff, 20; Newscom: agefotostock/Ton Koene, 19; Shutterstock: 1Roman Makedonsky, 13, Andrea Izzotti, 26, DGLimages, 5, Felix Lipov, 27, gary yim, 10, Homo Cosmicos, 16, Igor Grochev, 21, Jarun Ontakrai, 28, John And Penny, 6, Jon Chica, 17, Julie Scheveneels, 7, Luke Schmidt, Cover, MawardiBahar, 8, Nejdet Duzen, 1, Olena Tur, 18, orangecrush, 23, SIHASAKPRACHUM, 15, Subodh Agnihotri, 11, Sylvie Corriveau, 9, Wiangderm, 25, Wright Out There, 22. Design elements: Capstone; Shutterstock: Stawek (map), VLADGRIN.

Every effort has been made to contact copyright holders of material reproduced in this book. Any omissions will be rectified in subsequent printings if notice is given to the publisher.

All the internet addresses (URLs) given in this book were valid at the time of going to press. However, due to the dynamic nature of the internet, some addresses may have changed, or sites may have changed or ceased to exist since publication. While the author and publisher regret any inconvenience this may cause readers, no responsibility for any such changes can be accepted by either the author or the publisher.

CONTENTS

There's no place like home 4

From country to city 6

On the move 12

Hot and cold 16

Under and over 20

Important houses 24

Map 29

Glossary 30

Find out more 31

Index 32

Words in **bold** are in the glossary.

THERE'S NO PLACE LIKE HOME

A home is a safe place to stay. It keeps us out of bad weather. It's where we rest. It's where we spend time with family. What is special about your home?

Around the world, people build many types of homes. Some are made with mud. Others are made with **concrete**. Some are built close together, and others are far apart. No matter what, there's no place like home!

FROM COUNTRY TO CITY

Where is your home? Some homes are in the **country**. They have lots of land around them.

Country homes are often made with material that is easy to find. In Ireland, some are built with stones. The roof is thick straw.

Irish country homes are often painted white.

Rondavel houses in South Africa

In South Africa, stones are used to build *rondavel* homes. A mix of water and soil holds them together. Some people cover the stones with cow **dung**. After it dries, the house is painted bright colours.

A **suburb** is an area just outside a **city**. Homes in suburbs are close to each other.

In some countries, the homes are laid out neatly. Streets are set up in a pattern. Houses line each one. The homes in Malaysia are often built in rows. They share walls.

A suburb in Malaysia

Homes in Haiti

In other places, suburban homes are packed very close together. In Haiti, some houses fill the side of a mountain. Many have roofs made of metal.

Cities are busy places. Some have millions of people. There is not always a lot of space to build, so a common city home is an **apartment**. There are many apartments in one building.

The largest apartment building in the world is in Brazil. It has more than 1,000 apartments! More than 5,000 people live inside it.

The world's largest apartment building

Apartment buildings in India

Apartments can be big. But they can also be very small inside. In India and other places, some apartments have only one room.

ON THE MOVE

What if you need to live in more than one place? Then you can have a home that can be moved.

One type of house that can be moved is a houseboat. It floats on water like a boat. But it has many of the same parts as a house on land. It has places to cook, sleep and relax.

People in Canada often keep their houseboats next to each other. The homes make a floating **neighbourhood**.

Houseboats in Canada can have more than one floor.

In some **cultures**, people often move from place to place. They are called **nomads**. Some travel to find work. Others look for food for themselves or for their animals. Nomads take their homes with them on each move.

Nomads in Mongolia have gers. These homes are large, round tents made from sheep's wool. They can be put up quickly. The tent parts are also easy to pack and move.

Gers have wooden doors painted with colourful patterns.

HOT AND COLD

What is the weather like where you live? Some parts of the world are very hot. Homes need to stay cool inside.

Some people in Niger live in **huts**. The walls are built from clay. The roofs are made from straw. Both keep out the heat.

Homes in Niger built with clay

A courtyard

Homes in Morocco may have a **courtyard**. This is an open space in the middle of a house. It doesn't have a roof. This lets cool air move through the rooms.

Other parts of the world are very cold. Homes need to keep people warm.

In Norway, some homes have grass growing on the roof! The grass helps keep in heat.

A roof with grass growing on it is called a sod roof.

An Inuit man builds an igloo.

Another cold weather home is an igloo. It's made from blocks of snow. It's used for short amounts of time. Some Inuit people in Canada, Greenland and Alaska build igloos while on hunting trips. Then they are safe from the wind and cold.

UNDER AND OVER

Would you live underground? For some it makes sense. The earth keeps the home from getting too hot or cold.

In Australia, there is a town called Coober Pedy. It's mostly underground! Many homes are dug into the hillsides.

An underground home in Coober Pedy

A cave home in Tunisia

Some people in Tunisia live in cave homes. They dig a large hole deep into the ground. Then they cut out rooms from the sides of the hole.

Would you like to live off the ground? In some places, homes are built on **stilts**. These poles raise up a house. In Vietnam, it can rain a lot. So homes are often put on stilts to keep them safe from flooding.

Stilts raise some homes in Vietnam.

Beach houses in Bermuda

Other people build stilt homes to be close to water. They can live near rivers, lakes and oceans. On the island of Bermuda, many homes are right on the beach!

IMPORTANT HOUSES

Leaders sometimes live in special homes. These places may be big. They may be important to a country.

Some of these homes are very old. Windsor Castle has been a home to British kings and queens for about a thousand years! People who work for the royal family live there too. People from all over the world can come to visit. Can you imagine living in a home like that?

People visiting Windsor Castle

Other leaders only stay in special houses while they have their jobs. They live and work there.

The president of the United States lives in the White House in Washington D.C. It has 6 floors and more than 130 rooms, including a blowling alley, a cinema and a swimming pool.

The president lives and works in the White House.

Jubilee House

Ghana's president lives in the Jubilee House. It looks like a stool. For many years, Ghana's leaders sat on a special stool. The building's shape honours that **custom**.

Some people live in old homes. Other people build new houses. But one thing is the same. Homes are special places where we live our lives. What type of home would you like?

MAP

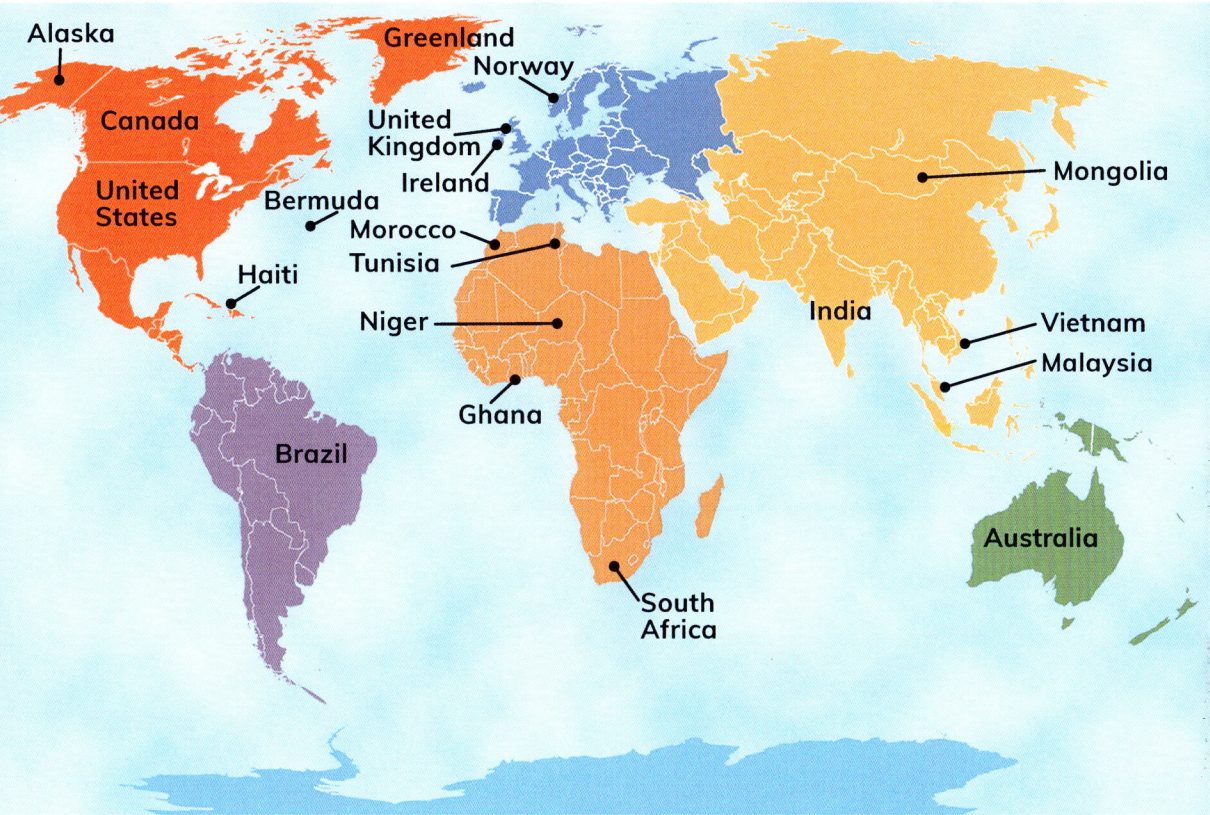

Around the world, people live in different homes. See which places were talked about in this book!

GLOSSARY

apartment another word for a flat; one of many homes in a building with its own rooms and front door

city area in which many people live and work that is larger than a town

concrete mix of cement, water, sand and gravel that hardens when it dries

country land that is away from towns and cities and has few buildings

courtyard open space in the middle of a building

culture group of people's way of life

custom usual way of doing something in a place or for a group of people

dung solid waste from animals

hut small home built from natural materials such as clay and straw

neighbourhood small area within a bigger place where people live

nomad person who moves from place to place instead of living in one spot

suburb area just outside a city, usually with many homes and fewer businesses

FIND OUT MORE

BOOKS

Home Life Through the Years: How Daily Life Has Changed in Living Memory (History in Living Memory), Clare Lewis (Raintree, 2016)

National Trust: Step Inside Homes Through History, Goldie Hawk (Nosy Crow, 2019)

This is My Home, Angela Royston (Raintree, 2019)

WEBSITES

www.bbc.co.uk/bitesize/articles/z8693j6
Learn more about homes in the snow.

www.dkfindout.com/uk/history/castles
Find out about living in a castle!

INDEX

apartments 10, 11
Australia 20

Bermuda 23
Brazil 10
building materials 4, 6, 7, 9, 14, 16, 19

Canada 12, 19
cities 8, 10
country homes 6
courtyards 17
cultures 14
customs 27

Ghana 27

Haiti 9
houseboats 12
huts 16

igloos 19
India 11
Inuit 19
Ireland 6

Jubilee House 27

leaders 24, 26, 27

Malaysia 8
Mongolia 14
Morocco 17

Niger 16
nomads 14
Norway 18

roofs 6, 9, 16, 17, 18
rooms 11, 17, 21, 26

South Africa 7
stilts 22, 23
suburbs 8, 9

tents 14
Tunisia 21

underground 20
United States 26

Vietnam 22

walls 8, 16
water 7, 12, 22, 23
weather 4, 16, 18, 19, 22
White House 26
Windsor Castle 24